Ditch the Bucket List and Live NOW

A memoir and workbook for those wanting to live life with purpose and passion.

Carolyn Manning-Washington, Ed.D.

Proverbs 3
**Before opening this memoir and guide, read Proverbs 3
as your guide for wisdom and well-being.**

For what is your life? It is even a vapor that appears for a little time and then vanishes away. -James 4:14

Life has afforded all of us time to reflect, focus, change and grow.

Time has permitted me to work on this piece during the COVID19 pandemic, a time in which the entire nation has been placed in quarantine, individuals are spending more time alone, and people are assessing their current spiritual, physical, mental, and financial situations.

I pray that you are using this time for self-reflecting and that you become a better you in 2020.

This memoir and workbook is written
"for such a time as this" and in honor of the Manning Family.

Written and Published in honor of the 9th year anniversary of the loss of my mother Gearldine Herron Manning-Malone.

To whom much is given much is required !

Reflection and Purpose

The bird that speaks intentionally to growth and change is the Sankofa bird taken from African mythology.

The Sankofa bird flies with its head facing backward with a proverbial meaning translating as "it is not wrong to go back for that which you have forgotten and bring forward that which is useful".

It is my prayer that you decide today is the day to reflect and bring forward those things that bring hope and the promise of the abundant life that God has for you.

Dr. C

CONTENTS

The Realities

Introduction

Reality 1: Tomorrow is not Promised

Reality 2: Nobody owes you anything

Reality 3: Everything does not NEED to be perfectly-planned

Reality 4: While in your "Meantime"

Reality 5: Live your life and stop making excuses

Reality 6: Let it Go !

Reality 7: Plan to prosper

Reality 8: Settle all the scores

Reality 9: Defeated dreamer. Get up!

Reality 10: All things work together for good
Summary

"For I know the plans I have for you declares the Lord, "plans to prosper you and not harm you, plans to give you hope and a future".

Jeremiah 29:11

Introduction

You have likely heard the question or made the statement many times before and perhaps even in the past week. Here is the question and statement "Is that on your bucket list? or statement "that's on my bucket list". For some reason this well-used catch question/phrase has been around for eternity. As a matter of fact, it is so frequently used that I believe that we subconsciously move this thought pattern to other areas of our lives without even knowing it. Not only do I believe that this has perpetuated poor choices, no choices and even discarded or failed choices and actions, I further believe that it has hindered growth in one way or another.

Remember the poem by Langston Hughes, "what happens to a dream deferred?", well my friend, I'm afraid to tell you that most dreams get left on the bucket list and never materialize. Dreams, plans, goals, ideas stuck right there in the bucket of our minds.

In a day and time when unprecedented things are happening at an alarming rate, this book will hopefully assist you in identifying some or all of the reasons why you might want to **STOP** putting things on a bucket list! In fact, if you stop and really think about what a bucket is really designed for, it might baffle you as to why many people have continued to use this phrase with very little thought. So just for a minute think about what buckets are made for and jot down your answer below. List it, write it, I'm not grading it. It's just an opportunity for you to brainstorm. After all it is your book, you have paid for it ☺

_____

_____

_____

_____

_____

_____

You likely came up with answers such as: buckets are made for keeping, storing, collecting, containing and gathering. Or maybe you came up with some other creative answer. But the reality is that most of the time when we place something in a bucket it usually stays there forever and we often either trash it or it ends up being transferred to another bucket.

Today, and in the days to come, I would like to challenge you with the thought that "Buckets are meant to be poured out, drained, emptied and even discarded", yes many of us are continuing to add things to our bucket list of life and now the buckets are overflowing with a bunch of unused ideas, poor habits, negativity and even unhealthy relationships. It is high-time to assess some possible realities of the mess and stuff in the bucket, evaluate your personal mishaps, learn a new thought, resolve and commit to a different and more positive approach.

This is a working piece where you will have an opportunity as part of your evolution in thinking to check out the realities, journal, reflect on positive messages or quotes, remember words of affirmation to access when you find yourself reverting to old ways and make a verbal resolution that will seal the deal psychologically.

I am by no means chalking this up to a quick-fix, this is merely a little bit of self-help for those of us who have accumulated more "bucket list" than we ever imagined, for those that didn't even know they were carrying buckets, and for those in denial about their buckets.

Activities: Use this as a workbook and set aside perhaps a week to go through and reflect on each chapter. Read the scriptures and be intentional in completing each section. Each Reality Check includes the following sections, work through each section and you are sure to find yourself developing your Christian values.

Quickwrite (assess)

Reflection (think)

Remember (affirmation)

Resolve (speak it)

Refer (Gods promise):

Special Note: Throughout this book you will read stories, all names mentioned are pseudonyms given to protect privacy and identity.

So, go on turn the page and start reading the top ten reasons why YOU need to "ditch the bucket list" and do it right now!

Funny yet TRUE story:

Confession of how this book stayed in a bucket on my computer for 7 years.

August 8, 1994 the writing of this book was revealed to me on a plane ride to Memphis, Tn. I can't for the life of me remember why or how the thought initiated, but I remember brainstorming a truckload of notes on my cell phone the entire trip. Today, I still have this brainstorming list in my phone, of which I referred to today when I decided I was kicking the bucket and publishing this book.

Fast forward, May 25, 2017 I open the notes and begin putting thoughts on paper and turning these thoughts into something tangible. Developing short chapters at a time and periodically adding a thought and most of all praying for what God wanted me to do with this piece.

I now sit in the middle of a pandemic on August 20, 2020 (also the 9th year anniversary of my mothers passing), and God has revealed to me that it is time to get this piece out of the bucket!
Bless my heart.

From the inception of this idea to now, many major events have taken place in my life. I share them as a reflection of God's work and also as a reminder of my journey.

- Went through a divorce, Lost my mother and a brother
- Resigned from my job to become an entrepreneur
- Lived internationally and traveled extensively
- Shifted to a minimalist mindset

- Successfully defended my dissertation and earned the degree of Doctor of Education
- Grew closer to God
- Experienced faith and peace that surpasses all understanding

"Be strong and courageous. Do not be afraid or terrified because of them, for the Lord your God goes with you, he will never leave you nor forsake you" Deuteronomy 3:16

REALITY ONE
Tomorrow is not promised!

Tomorrow is not promised! we know this in theory, and we see it in reality daily. Not only is this a biblical principle, it is a fact of life. How many people do you know that start a great deal of sentences with, "when I get on my feet", "when things are better for me", or even the phrase, I'll get around to it".

The bible tells us that "life is a vapor that appears for a little while and then vanishes away! Either we don't have a clue what a vapor is, or we simply have not processed the concept of vaporization. In either case I believe we hear this statement and somehow drop it perhaps in the bucket list of our minds as something we will get back to. The gut-wrenching reality is that life really is a vapor! So, you better get going before you vapor has dissolved. I don't mean to intentionally throw this out as a harsh fact…well, yes, I do; because for the most part I believe that most people are running around thinking that they really have a lease on life and will be here forever. Well if the reality hadn't hit by now, open your local news and you will see the startling numbers of the number of lives lost to COVID19.

It's time for a reality check:

Check This:

- ✓ Jaime 16 years old goes to the doctor to find out that that she has a debilitating illness and is told she has six months to live
- ✓ Shawn a mother of three, has been married for fifteen years and in one year she becomes a divorcee and unemployed

- ✓ Genesis a minister's wife believes she has found her soul mate only to discover that he is mating with another male
- ✓ Devin a smart educated male with degrees from higher education institutions finds himself jobless and homeless
- ✓ Jason a young man on his way to college and hit by a drunk driver finds himself paralyzed from the waist down
- ✓ Cindy in an effort to maintain a more physically fit body strains a muscle, damages nerves while working with her trainer and continuous to deal with periodic pain.
- ✓ Jennifer a healthy senior who has never been ill and has led a very self-sustaining life goes for a routine checkup only to find out that she has breast cancer which results in a mastectomy.

I could go on and on with so many more real-life situations, as these are situations that have occurred in my small circle; with names changed for confidentiality of course. But I think you get the point. Point being, that we are living life day to day with zero control of what will happen. Zero, that means none, nada, simply put "you" cant control anything.! Have you truly internalized this?

Write (assess): Write one thing in the space below that you have a desire to do, be or achieve. Don't take too long as this is intended to be a quick-thinking activity. Research shows that the first thought that comes to mind is typically more closely associated with your true intention.

_____

_____.

Reflection (think): Now write one paragraph about what you want to do and include who you would do this with, etc.

_____

_____

_____

_____

_____

_____

_____

_____.

Remember (affirmation): Repeat this thought throughout the day reminding yourself of the sanctity of embracing all that today offers:

* ❖ *Today I will live my life in such a way that I bring peace to all I come in contact with.*

Resolve (speak it): Read this aloud to yourself as a resolution to again embrace all that today offers:

- I resolve today to live each day as though it is my last. To live a life that is committed to love, joy, peace, service and happiness. I resolve to do so because I recognize that life is a vapor and that time beyond this very moment is not promised. I will no longer put off that which continues to dwell in my spirit. I will acknowledge even the very thought of someone entering my mind at a specific moment as a moment for me to maximize my vapor and to reach out to this person.

Refer (Gods promise): Reflect on Gods promise for this reading taken from: Matthew 6:34

- "Take therefore no thought for tomorrow: for tomorrow shall take thought for the things of itself"

REALITY TWO
Nobody owes you anything

Entitlement! The term given to this current generation and perhaps one that permeates throughout the nation. Society has somehow instilled the idea that someone owes us something. No I'm not talking about 40 acres and a mule (that could be argued with certainty). I am talking about ideas such as: everyone wins a trophy, even when the last kid came across the finish line twenty minutes later, or seven year old's walking around with cell phones, and perhaps even leaders of the country sometimes feeling like they can use their executive power to make decisions just because "they can". Gone are the days of individuals staying on jobs until retirement, in fact it is well known that the millennials of the day seek opportunities that align closely with their personal ideology of showing up late, leaving early, and deciding whether the job provides good life-work balance.

I am not saying that any of this is wrong or counterproductive (as long as the work gets done) what I am saying is a switch must be turned off relative to the idea of "you being owed something" by family, friends, employers or anyone else.

We must all take account of our own thoughts, actions, and decisions and not hold anyone accountable for things they didn't do to help us get to the next step – maybe they were STUCK in their own steps and couldn't figure out how to move forward.

Write (assess): What is something that you think someone owed you that might have made a difference in your life had they come through. Don't take too long as this is intended to be a quick-thinking activity. Research shows that the first thought that comes to mind is typically more closely associated with your true intention.

_____

_____.

Reflection (think): Now write one paragraph forgiving them for not being available for you and another paragraph that releases them from this responsibility.

_____

_____

_____

_____

_____

_____

_____.

Remember (affirmation): Repeat this thought throughout the day reminding yourself of the sanctity of embracing all that today offers:

- ❖ *I embrace today for what it is – Life! And take ownership for the decisions I make in my life.*

Resolve (speak it): Read this aloud to yourself as a resolution to again embrace all that today offers:

- ♦ I resolve today to forgive and release anyone who might not have come through for me the way that I thought they should have. I don't know what that person was going through, how they came to understand life in the way that they did or did not, but at this moment they are released.

- ♦ Feel free to write and speak aloud the names of those you forgive and release:

- ♦ I forgive and release ___ for _____

- ♦ I forgive and release ___ for _____

- ♦ I forgive and release ___ for _____

Refer (Gods promise): Reflect on Gods promise for this reading taken from *Ephesians 4:31-32*

- "Get rid of all bitterness, rage, and anger, brawling and slander, along with every form of malice. Be kind and compassionate to one another, forgiving each other, just as Christ God forgave you"

REALITY THREE
Everything does not NEED to be perfectly-planned

Give God some credit will you! I am convinced that our father is the greatest planner ever. He planned the world and all that was formed, he created and planned babies, he designed the most beautiful of all beings and he planned his own suffering to save us. We have the master planner!

So often what prevents us from moving forward is that we are so busy thinking about doing something, but never getting beyond the thinking or talking phase. How many times have you said "I am going to go to back to college to finish my degree", "I am going to start working out", and here is one "I am going back to church as soon as I get it all together" (well I can save you some time on this one…you will never have it ALL together).

What helped me. A few years ago, I adopted a new mindset that goes like this: If I am thinking about doing something, I follow this thought with prayer and fasting, and challenge myself to start in a small way. Wouldn't you know that for most things I started...I actually finished.

The example: Early 2016 I started thinking about returning to school to work on my doctorate. I prayed about it, asked a few others to join me in prayer. By summer of 2016 I still wasn't convinced that I wanted to commit to the work for the next several years. Here is what I told myself "take one or two classes and see how you feel. If you like it continue. If you don't like it come up with a new plan"

Outcome: I thoroughly enjoyed my courses, stayed the course and obtained my Doctorate in Education, July 2020. None of this would have happened had I waited on the perfect plan, perfect time, or perfect season or the money.

Sometimes we have to just MOVE on it!

Write (assess): What is something that you have been talking about or thinking about doing for a long time and you just haven't acted on it because you just haven't planned it out perfectly. Don't take too long as this is intended to be a quick-thinking activity. Research shows that the first thought that comes to mind is typically more closely associated with your true intention.

_____

_____.

Reflection (think): Now write two steps you could take to MOVE on this Goal. Also, identify 2 people that could serve as accountability and prayer partners:

_____

_____
_____
_____
_____
_____
_____
_____.

Remember (affirmation): Repeat this thought throughout the day reminding yourself of the sanctity of embracing all that today offers:

- ❖ *God has plans for me – it's my MOVE !*

Resolve (speak it): Read this aloud to yourself as a resolution to again embrace all that today offers:

- ✦ I resolve today to pray that God will reveal his plans for me. He is the master planner and through prayer I will follow his lead toward my desires and dreams.

Refer (Gods promise): Reflect on Gods promise for this reading taken from *Jeremiah 29:11*

- "For I know the plans I have for you, declares the Lord, plans to prosper you and not to harm you, plans to give you hope and a future".

REALITY FOUR
While in your Meantime

In the Meantime? This is the time when you are in what I call a holding pattern. You may be in between a job, in between relationships, in between choices, or just in a holding pattern. This is a space where God is calling for you to be still and hear from him. This is the space and time before something happens or before a specific period is ending.

So many of us are used to ripping, running, and being in a rat race that it is difficult to embrace your MEANTIME.

I have experienced some of the most amazing thoughts, met the most inspirational people, and traveled to some amazing places while in my meantime. The key was to just allow yourself to "BE in the present" so that you could hear from God.

Here are some helpful ideas:

- When in your meantime **PRAY**
- When in your meantime **Set Goals**
- When in your meantime **Listen**
- When in your meantime **Be Still**
- When in your meantime **Wait**
- When in your meantime **Serve**

One of my most reflective "Meantime" experiences was taking a five-day cruise alone. I had never cruised alone and was a bit apprehensive walking into this experience. The first person I met was a beautiful heavy set African-American woman who I will refer to as "big momma angel". She was eighty years old and had the prettiest long pigtails on each side of her head and a smile that lit up the ship. We seemed to cross paths each morning during breakfast and she would tell me stories of her life and laugh about how long her 70-year old husband was taking in the bathroom. She exuded wisdom, knowledge, kindness, and a strength that drew me in each morning. She would catch me on the deck reading "The Power of NOW" and often ask me to share with her my readings. I enjoyed every moment with this beautiful queen and left with wisdom beyond my years from the lady with the long gray pigtails. I am sure I may never cross her path again – but in my "MEANTIME" she was my messenger of hope, encouragement, and life. My job was to stop long enough each morning to just say hello.

Write (assess): Are you in a "MeanTime" or know someone that is? If you are, use this space to assess why you believe you are in this holding pattern and write a prayer for God to reveal to you his purpose for you during this season. Don't take too long as this is intended to be a quick-thinking activity. Research shows that the first thought that comes to mind is typically more closely associated with your true intention.

_____

_____.

Reflection (think): Write about a time recently that you have had a MEANTIME experience. How did you use this time? what would you do differently when you are in a holding pattern in the future?

_____

_____

_____

_____

_____

_____

_____

Remember (affirmation): Repeat this thought throughout the day reminding yourself of the sanctity of embracing all that today offers:

- ❖ *I accept my MEANTIME experience and am allowing God to reveal to me his purpose.*

Resolve (speak it): Read this aloud to yourself as a resolution to again embrace all that today offers:

- ✚ I resolve today to accept my MEANTIME experience. I am more than a conqueror in Christ Jesus. As I end one season or as a new season begin's I embrace the change as part of my divine journey.

Refer (Gods promise): Reflect on Gods promise for this reading taken from *Psalms 46:10 and Ecclesiastes 3:1*

- ✚ "Be still, and know that I am God; I will be exalted among the nations, I will be exalted in the earth"
- ✚ "There is a time for everything, and a season for every activity under the heavens.

REALITY FIVE
Live your Life and Stop making Excuses

There is always a reason to not do something. Excuses have been around as far back as Adam blaming Eve and the dog eating the homework. Whatever excuses you've had...drop them today.

Here are some of my previous excuse hostages:

- It's just too hot to go outside and exercise
- That's a long way to drive
- I am just not in the mood
- I get up everyday for work, 8 am on Sunday just feels too early
- I just don't have the money

Well, I had to come to the reality that I was making these excuses for one or two reasons: "I really didn't want to do something" or "I was just simply too lazy to follow through" in either case the first step is to **OWN the Why!**

Over the years I have come to realize that when a person wants to do something, go somewhere, or be involved they will make it happen no matter what, it simply boils down to whether they **WANT** to do it or not.

Write (assess): Own your WHY! Is there something you know you need to change to help you live life more effectively? If so, own them and write them down now. Don't take too long as this is intended to be a quick-thinking activity. Research shows that the first thought that comes to mind is typically more closely associated with your true intention.

_____

_____.

Reflection (think): Now write one paragraph forgiving yourself for making excuses and choose one or two of these life changing activities and write a plan of action to move forward in a positive way (losing weight, engaging with others, participating in church, making healthy choices). Healthy choices lead to healthy living.

_____

_____

_____

_____

_____

_____

_____

_____

_____.

Remember (affirmation): Repeat this thought throughout the day reminding yourself of the sanctity of embracing all that today offers:

> ❖ *Today I will with confidence make time to do what is important for my mind, body and spirit as I focus on living a more intentional and healthy life.*

Resolve (speak it): Read this aloud to yourself as a resolution to again embrace all that today offers:

- I resolve today to live a no guilt, no shame, no excuses Life. Making improvements one day at a time with the help of the Lord.

Refer (Gods promise): Reflect on Gods promise for this reading taken from *Proverbs 6:4 and Exodus 4:10-14*

- "Don't put it off; do it now! Don't rest until you do"
- "But Moses pleaded with the Lord, "O Lord, I'm not very good with words. I never have been, and I'm not now, even though you have spoken to me. I get tongue-tied, and my words get tangled." Then the Lord asked Moses, "Who makes a person's mouth? Who decides whether people speak or do not speak, hear or do not hear, see or do not see? Is it not I, the Lord? Now go! I will be with you as you speak, and I will instruct you in what to say." But Moses again pleaded, "Lord, please! Send anyone else." Then the Lord became angry with Moses. "All right," he said. "What about your brother, Aaron the Levite? I know he speaks well. And look! He is on his way to meet you now. He will be delighted to see you."

REALITY SIX
Let it Go!

You know the melody "Oh what peace we often forfeit all because we do not carry everything to God in prayer!" this song has reminded me often to pray, not worry, and to trust that prayer changes things. We know the serenity prayer quite well, yet it is difficult to put these words into practice when hurt, pain, anger, deception, financial hardship, and loss are knocking at your door.

Serenity Prayer

"God grant me the serenity to accept the things I cannot change;

courage to change the things I can; and wisdom to know the

difference"

The longer we live the more we learn that God is in total control! For those of us still struggling with this and think we are running anything more than turning on water faucets - reflect for a moment on how COVID19 came in and changed the entire course of our nation, economy, schools, families, churches and many other aspects of life. COVID19 reminded all of us regardless of race, socioeconomic status, jobs, etc. **WE ARE NOT IN CONTROL! God is.**

Here is a testimony for you. In February 2020, I received a medical bill for almost $30,000. I did all the right things, took my insurance card, wrote letters, went back and forward with two agencies who refused to pay because of the way the hospital coded the visit. I was at a complete lost. I called the hospital and told them I didn't have the money and asked what adjustments or plans could be made. As

God is my witness and probably all of my neighbors because of my hallelujah dance and shout, on August 17, 2020 I received a letter saying my bill was paid in full! You hear me, PAID IN FULL. In fact, the letter said I owed in print **$0.00** - nothing the debt was completely eliminate! The letter further stated if I had made any payments that all money would be reimbursed.

Only God can make **MONEY MOVES** like this.

Write (assess): What is something that you are holding on to because you think you are in control? Wouldn't it be better to just release it to the Lord and let him handle it. Don't take too long as this is intended to be a quick-thinking activity. Research shows that the first thought that comes to mind is typically more closely associated with your true intention.

_____

_____.

Reflection (think): Now write one paragraph forgiving yourself for wanting to be in control of this matter and relinquish it to the Lord.

_____

_____

_____

_____

_____

_____

_____.

Remember (affirmation): Repeat this thought throughout the day reminding yourself of the sanctity of embracing all that today offers:

❖ *For your thoughts are not my thought, neither your ways my ways. I will trust your ways and thoughts Lord*

Resolve (speak it): Read this aloud to yourself as a resolution to again embrace all that today offers:

- I resolve today to relinquish my controlling attitude and controlling spirit. I know that God is walking before me and he only wants what is best for me. He is my strength and my salvation.

Refer (Gods promise): Reflect on Gods promise for this reading taken from *Deuteronomy 31:8*

- "The Lord himself goes before you and will be with you; he will never leave you nor forsake you. Do not be afraid; do not be discouraged"

REALITY SEVEN
Plan to prosper

Oh, how I love Gods promises! and the assurance that God never lies and always follows through. One of the promises that I have kept at my fingertips for as long as I remember has been God's plans for me to prosper. I decided a long time ago, if God planned for me to prosper than I better get on board and do my part.

How comforting it is that when God created me in my mothers' womb, he already had plans for me! Now this is a hallelujah moment. I don't know if you have truly sat back and though about what God planned for your life but today is that day!

Even on the days when you have no idea what you want to do, whether you still want to stay in your career, what steps to take to make a new move, find comfort in knowing that God already knows.

Not only does God already know, he has also promised to literally give us the DESIRES of our hearts! What a mighty God we serve. While writing this I began to reflect on my life and realized that everything I had prayed for that fell into the will of God's word and will – God has provided. I would encourage you to test the Lord and watch him come through.

Write (assess): What is one desire of your heart? Have you prayed to God about it? Don't take too long as this is intended to be a quick-thinking activity. Research shows that the first thought that comes to mind is typically more closely associated with your true intention.

_____

_____.

Reflection (think): Now write a prayer with the specific desires of your heart and pray that if it is God's will that these desires will manifest in your life.

_____
_____
_____
_____
_____
_____
_____
_____
_____.

Remember (affirmation): Repeat this thought throughout the day reminding yourself of the sanctity of embracing all that today offers:

- ❖ *God already made plans for me to prosper ! Thank you Lord!*

Resolve (speak it): Read this aloud to yourself as a resolution to again embrace all that today offers:

- I resolve today to give God my best knowing that he has already planned for me to prosper, has given me a spirit of hope embedded in a positive future. I am smart, I am intelligent, and I am ready to walk in victory.

Refer (Gods promise): Reflect on Gods promise for this reading taken from *Jeremiah 29:11and Malachi 3:11*

- "For I know the plans I have for you" declares the Lord, "plans to prosper you and not to harm you, plans to give you hope and a future"
- Bring the whole tithe into the storehouse, that there may be food in my house. Test me in this," says the LORD Almighty, "and see if I will not throw open the floodgates of heaven and pour out so much blessing that there will not be room enough to store it.

REALITY EIGHT
Settle all the scores

There is nothing in life more unsettling than the lack of forgiveness. Forgiveness is the gateway to life and our soul. It is through forgiveness that we stay connected to our Lord, as he showed us by his example of forgiving us even in the midst of our sins.

While forgiveness may mean different things for different people; what it means biblically is "to let go". There are also at least three biblical truths about forgiveness that are worthy of mentioning:

- All of us need forgiveness
- Forgiveness of others is a prerequisite for our own forgiveness
- Lack of forgiveness breaks our fellowship with God

Yes, I know, sometimes people treat us or have treated us in ways that we just simply can't find the strength to let go and forgive them. Trust me, I dare not minimize your experiences because I do not know the depth of what you are or have experienced. But what I know from experience is that lack of forgiveness will suffocate your soul and mind and keep you from performing at your maximum mental capacity.

When pain keeps us from forgiving this is where we need prayer to soften our spirits and hearts so we can walk in our full purpose. Pinned up emotions are detrimental to our minds, bodies and spirits. Robbing us of happiness and often leading to feelings of misery and distress. When our bodies experience such feelings in an ongoing manner it can lead to high levels of stress, blood pressure concerns, psychological and emotional concerns, and even alcohol and drug use.

When we extend our hearts through prayer and forgive, we are able to live in the bonds of peace and unity with all men and maintain a relationship with others and God. Others will see us extending ourselves beyond that which others could even imagine. Forgiveness does not mean forgetting, condoning or excusing the behavior – but forgiveness allows us through prayer to move forward in with our hearts at peace and we can truly experience "peace that passeth all understanding".

In my experience, one of my greatest challenges has been self-forgiveness. This too can hamper our progress and hold us hostage in our mind, body, and spirit. It is easy to forget that God has already nailed our sins to the cross, because it is difficult to perceive. However, the assurance comes in knowing that God is a forgiving God, not wanting anyone to perish but to have eternal life.

Note: If you are experiencing difficulty with forgiveness of self and/or others seek additional support through counseling , services with your employee assistance program, or check with your local church to see if they have a Christian counselor on staff. Sometimes the depth of pain is far deeper than that which can be addressed in this workbook.

Write (assess): Is there someone you are having a difficult time forgiving? If so, list their names here and begin praying that God will release you and bring you to a place of forgiveness. Don't take too long as this is intended to be a quick-thinking activity. Research shows that the first thought that comes to mind is typically more closely associated with your true intention.

_____
_____.

Reflection (think): Now write a prayer of forgiveness for this person.

_____

_____

_____

_____

_____

_____

_____

_____.

Remember (affirmation): Repeat this thought throughout the day reminding yourself of the sanctity of embracing all that today offers:

- ❖ *God demonstrated his love for me, that while I was in sin, Christ died for me.*

Resolve (speak it): Read this aloud to yourself as a resolution to again embrace all that today offers:

- I resolve today to forgive others as Christ has forgiven me and pray specifically for God to give me the strength to forgive those who I have struggled to forgive.

Refer (Gods promise): Reflect on Gods promise for this reading taken from *Psalms 103:8-12 and I Corinthians 13*

- The Lord is compassionate and gracious, slow to anger, abounding in love. He will not always accuse, nor will he harbor his anger forever; he does not treat us as our sins deserve or repay us according to our iniquities. For as high as the heavens are above the earth, so great is his love for those who fear him; as far as the east is from the west, so far has he removed our transgressions from us

- Bearing with one another and, if one has a complaint against another, forgiving each other, as the Lord has forgiven you, so you must also forgive. And above all these put on love, which binds everything together in perfect harmony.

REALITY NINE
Defeated dreamer, Get up

Have you ever lost a dream? felt like the time had passed for you to accomplish something? Have you found yourself in a woulda, coulda, shoulda space? Are you feeling regret for not reaching a certain point in your life at a certain time? Ever felt that you had fallen so far from grace that you would not be received by the Lord? Well, I believe in most of our lives we have felt a few of these feelings leaving us with unresolved guilt, shame, embarrassment and failure.

Guess what, today is your day to get back up again! Yes, another promise from God is that he provides comfort for us and he is ready to always receive us.

When I moved to Houston in 1991, the church I attended had a prolific speaker as a minister. His words, though country in accent were poised with a type of assurance that melted your soul. Every Sunday before he began his message, he would speak the following words from Matthew 11:28-29:

"Come unto me, all ye that labour and are heavy laden, and I will give you rest. Take my yoke upon you, and learn of me; for I am meek and lowly in heart: and ye shall find rest unto your souls"

This passage resonated so strongly with me as I had spent the previous four years in and out of hospitals and at times bedridden stricken with the debilitating pain of Systemic Lupus. While I didn't understand all of the passage, what I did understand was "I wanted rest for my soul". The hope that came through from one Sunday to the next was enough to give me the energy I needed to **GET BACK UP AGAIN!**

With the Lords help and through prayer and a supportive family I ran, and ran, and ran some more. It took me 10 years to complete my bachelor's degree, two more as I ran toward my masters, an attempt at a doctorate in counseling that I walked away from to serve my mother in her last days, and a return to a doctoral program in 2016 with a 2020 completion. **I got back up again and so can you!**

We are never too old to reach back and grab a dream. Just the other day I read online that an 80 year old man finished school, an 82 year old had earned the title of award-winning bodybuilder, and a 99 year old woman graduated from college. **It's time to Grab hold to your past dreams or create some new ones !**

Write (assess): What dream have you deferred? What steps are you willing to get up again and run toward your dreams? Don't take too long as this is intended to be a quick-thinking activity. Research shows that the first thought that comes to mind is typically more closely associated with your true intention.

_____

_____.

Reflection (think): Reflect on the poem "Choices" by Nikki Giovanni. What does this poem mean in your life.

Choices

if I can't do
what I want to do
then my job is to not
do what I don't want to do

it's not the same thing
but it's the best I can
do

if I cant have
what I want then

my job is to want
what I've got
and be satisfied
that at least there
is something more
to want

since i can't go
where i need
to go then i must go
where the signs point
though always understanding
parallel movement
isn't lateral

when i can't express
what i really feel
i practice feeling
what i can express
and none of it is equal
i know
but that's why mankind
alone among the animals
learns to cry

_____

_____

_____

_____

_____

_____

_____.

Remember (affirmation): Repeat this thought throughout the day reminding yourself of the sanctity of embracing all that today offers:

- ❖ *I can do all things through him who strengthens me*

Resolve (speak it): Read this aloud to yourself as a resolution to again embrace all that today offers:

- ✚ I resolve today to GET BACK UP AGAIN! and run toward my dreams. If I need help I will seek help through a mentor, life coach, or Christian advisor. It's time for me to Get BACK UP Again!

Refer (Gods promise): Reflect on Gods promise for this reading taken from *Philippians 4:13; Habakkuk 2:2-3; Proverbs 16:9*

- "I can do all things through him who strengthens me"
- "Write the vision, maki it plain on tablets, so he may run who reads it. For still the vision awaits its appointed time; it hastens to the end-it will not lie. If it seems slow, wait for it, it will surely come, it will not delay"
- "The hear of man plans his way, but the Lord establishes his steps"

REALITY TEN
All things work together for good

Another promise that God gives us is that "all things will work together for good". It is utterly impossible for us to comprehend the working of things for good in a world filled with so many societal ills, separatism, racism, legalism, sexism and all kinds of isms! But somehow God has promised us that all things will work together for good even in the absence of our understanding.

Wanna hear a story of things working for good? Put on your seatbelt and read this: In 2019 I moved internationally to work as a foreign principal. Excited about the opportunity I jumped in headfirst, arrived early, worked late, and embraced the new learning experience. What I was not prepared for was the intentional acts of those above me to schedule events and workdays on Sunday almost intentionally after I made it know that I would attend worship service on Sundays. While I held fast and attended early service so that I could also report to work, little did I know some were influenced by my commitment and wanted to know more about this place of worship (I still talk to many of the teachers that expressed the seed of love that was planted in the midst of a place that does not believe or acknowledge God).

In the midst of navigating my daily work, I received a call that the company was cutting back and I, along with three others from the states would no longer be needed in the position for which we have traveled across the globe. We were given one-week notice (remember I was 17 hours away from home!). I didn't call home to tell my family, they would have been scared, worried and sick. No what I did was Be Still and Pray for three days. And all the while I was praying and sleeping, God was planning a major move for me to join an entirely different organization in a little place called Tongzho, China (15 minutes from the Beijing International airport) as project manager (another moment to shout).

Check this out: housing and utilities were provided, I didn't have to work on Sunday, I worked fewer hours, got paid more and was nowhere near COVID19 when it started. An even greater God move that I didn't see coming was how God navigated this change in such a way that I was able to return to the states with my family before the COVID19 quarantine. All the while God was working to make it all for GOOD! My items are still secured internationally, I continued to receive pay for about six months, I was extended the opportunity to continue international work while being home with family, and I was given time to complete my doctorate! As we say at church **"Won't he do it"**. Again, God was moving the parts so that they would all work out for Good.

When we can't trace him…we simply must TRUST him !

On another note and a call to stand:

I would be remiss to write this memoir and not acknowledge the importance of Black Lives Matter and the movement toward justice for all that is ever-present as I am writing. Senseless deaths such as George Floyd, Michael Brown, Tamir Rice, Eric Garner, Sandra Bland, Breonna Taylor, Trayvon Martin and many others are strewn across our television screens as readily as they were in the 1960's. In the midst of such hideous acts, the U.S. is burdened with the lack of respect and the poor decisions that are made in the highest governmental offices.

With hope and prayer, we as a society and most important as individuals are called to find our place, find our lane and stand up for a democracy that supports justice for all.

In other words, we must walk the walk and speak up for those who are unable to speak up for themselves. Knowing that all things work together for good, even when we can't seem to find the good with our naked eye.

Write (assess): How can you become involved at the local level to support civic causes and to contribute to standing up for societal ills? Don't take too long as this is intended to be a quick-thinking activity. Research shows that the first thought that comes to mind is typically more closely associated with your true intention.

_____

_____.

Reflection (think): Now make a list of your local representatives and commit to getting involved. Maybe you can make phone calls, help with mail-outs, attend local events, or prayer. Whatever it is, find your lane and Get involved.

_____

_____

_____

_____

_____

_____

_____

_____.

Remember (affirmation): Repeat this thought throughout the day reminding yourself of the sanctity of embracing all that today offers:

- ❖ *Lord help me to live so that those who do not know you, will come to know you because they know me.*

Resolve (speak it): Read this aloud to yourself as a resolution to again embrace all that today offers:

- ✢ I resolve today to be an example amongst my fellow man, to serve when I see a need, and to pray for those who lead our country.

Refer (Gods promise): Reflect on Gods promise for this reading taken from ***Romans 8:28***

- ✢ "And we know that in all things God works for the good of those who love him, who have been called according to his purpose"

Summary

As you have worked through the Reality Checks in this booklet, I hope that you have began the process of getting rid of your bucket list and getting back to the work at hand. The work of trusting God with your life.

In the previous chapters I pointed out areas that tend to get in the way of our spiritual, mental, personal and professional progress. Whether male or female we are all challenged in areas that seem to take us off course from time to time.

One way to get on course is to reflect over your life as I have done in this memoir and remember just how gracious God has been and continues to be in your life. We all have memoirs, we just need to take time and reflect on some of them so that we will stay STRONG in the Lord.

Write (assess): If I missed an area in your life that you know you need to work on jot it down here and pray for God to walk you through the process of getting this out of your psychological bucket list.

Don't take too long as this is intended to be a quick-thinking activity. Research shows that the first thought that comes to mind is typically more closely associated with your true intention.

Reflection (think): Now write one paragraph reflecting on the previous activities and establish a plan for those areas that you still need to work on. Use this space to also set goals and to monitor your progress.

Remember (affirmation): Create your own affirmation(s) on the line below. Hang affirmations in your home, your car, at your desk. Visibility with help you stay centered:

❖

Resolve (speak it): Write your own personal resolve statement and use it as a guide to keep you centered and focus. Perhaps develop a resolve statement to reflect your spiritual, personal, health and financial goals

- (Spiritual) I resolve today to

- (Personal) I resolve today to

- (Health) I resolve today to

- (Health) I resolve today to

Refer (Gods promise): Reflect on Gods promise for this reading taken from *Matthew 21:22*

- "And whatever you ask in prayer, you will receive, if you have faith"

Ephesians 3:20 (New International Version)

Now unto him who is able to do immeasurably more than all we ask or imagine, according to his power that is at work within us.

In Jesus Name,

Amen

www.ingramcontent.com/pod-product-compliance
Lightning Source LLC
Chambersburg PA
CBHW041403090426
42743CB00006B/141